Twelve Stories
You and Your Children
Need to Know

Twelve Stories You and Your Children Need to Know

Values and Hope for a New Generation

William Hockin

Anglican Book Centre
Toronto, Canada

1994
Anglican Book Centre
600 Jarvis Street
Toronto, Ontario
M4Y 2J6

Canadian Cataloguing in Publication Data

Hockin, William J.

    Twelve stories you and your children need to know : finding hope for a new generation in the biblical story

ISBN 1-55126-110-3

1. Bible stories, English. I. Title

BS550.2.H63 1994   220.9'505   C94-932329-2

Acknowledgements

Page 12 — from *God's Trombones* by James Weldon Johnson, copyright © 1929. Used by permission of Harper Collins.

Page 14 — from acceptance speech for the Templeton Prize for Religion, copyright © 1983. Used by permission of the Templeton Prize.

Page 71 — from *Tell Me Again, Lord, I Forget* by Ruth Harms Calkin, copyright © 1974. Used by permission of Tyndale House Publishers Inc. All rights reserved.

Page 85 — "Little Gidding" from "Four Quartets" in *Collected Poems 1909 – 1962* by T. S. Eliot, copyright © 1963. Used by permission of Faber and Faber Ltd.

Contents

To Desmond C. Hunt

in deep gratitude

for a good friend and mentor

who loved the Story

and spent his life

making it come alive

for others

Preface

In spite of the title, this is not a collection of stories for children. It is, instead, a new look at Bible stories that we, their parents and grandparents, need to understand, so that we can retell the stories and the vital truths they convey.

Not very long ago, most people in the Western world knew or understood the basics of the stories about Moses and the Burning Bush, David and Goliath, the Golden Calf, the Prodigal Son, and the Good Samaritan. These stories are filled with precept, hope, mystery, and even excitement. But society seems not to value these stories as much as in the past — our collective memory for them, and the truths they contain, has become weak. There are fewer people who tell them and fewer people who hear them. There is, frankly, a lot of competition in the marketplace of ideas.

We are raising a generation without access to some of the greatest stories ever told. It is difficult for these stories to receive a hearing and take imaginative hold when only about fifteen per cent of the children in our public schools go to Sunday School. To make matters worse, it is likely that many parents of the current generation have missed the relevance of the stories as well.

I call this collection *Twelve Stories You and Your Children Need to Know* because I am convinced that these Bible stories are unique in human literature. They contain certain truths that we need in order to understand what life is about. These truths speak about the mystery of life, the sanctity of life, the virtues of life. And these truths come from God. That is why our children *need* to know, hear, and understand these stories.

Acknowledgements

To the people of St. Paul's, Bloor Street, Toronto
— for their gifts of time and encouragement
in this project.

To Jim MacLean, my editor and friend,
who made "rough places plain" and
"flowers grow in desert places."

To my wife and best friend, Isabelle,
for her encouragement and
long hours of keyboarding.

All Things Bright and Beautiful

*In the beginning . . . God created the heavens and the earth . .
. And God saw everything that he had made, and indeed, it
was very good.*

(Genesis 1:1, 31)

The American poet, James Weldon Johnson, in his book *God's Trombones*, attempted to recreate some of the great power and beauty of an old-time black preacher's sermon on creation. Here's what he wrote.

And God stepped out on space,
And he looked around and said:
I'm lonely —
I'll make me a world.
And as far as the eye of God could see
Darkness covered everything
Blacker than a hundred midnights
Down in a cypress swamp.
Then God smiled,
And the light broke,
And the darkness rolled up on one side,
And the light stood shining on the other,
And God said: That's good!
Then God reached out and took the light in his hands,
Until he made the sun;
And he set the sun a-blazing in the heavens.
And the light that was left over from making the sun
God gathered it up in a shining ball
And flung it against the darkness,
Spangling the night with moon and stars.
Then down between
The darkness and the light
He hurled the world;
And God said: That's good.

Everyone of us, at some point in our lives, asks How! How did life begin? Where did I really come from? Why am I me? How did the world get made? And the loudest replies seem to come from science. The laboratories of the planet produce theories — the evolution theory, the big

bang theory, the steady state theory, the chaos theory —
and no doubt, as science "progresses," there will be more.

The book of Genesis is not, of course, scientific theory.
Like the work of Johnson, it is inspired poetry. And, after
all, poetry is the best kind of language to describe the real
mysteries of existence — the mysteries of love, death, order, and beauty — indeed, the mystery of life itself.

Despite the ongoing debate between evolutionists and
creationists, there need be no conflict between science
and religion on this issue. Scientific research and theory
are essential to our lives, our understanding, and our survival. But man cannot live on theory alone, because we
ask more than just How, When, and What? We also ask
Why, Who, and What does it all mean? It is for those of
us who ask these questions that the Bible is written, and
especially chapter one of Genesis.

The first question that Genesis responds to is Who?
Who made the robin? Who made the pumpkin? Who
made me? If anyone says, "Those are pointless questions,
because there is no way of finding a definite answer," we
can reply, "That may be true, but one cannot help asking
the questions, because life keeps asking them of us." Is
life just a process that got started by some chemical acci-
dent, a process that will continue until some fool comes
along with a weapon able to destroy it forever? Or is there
something more than that? Genesis answers, "In the beginning, God created."

The first truth, therefore, that we hear from the story
of creation is this — there is a Who. The beginning verse
of Genesis establishes that we are not set adrift in some
mindless universe. Its creator is God, our Father.

In 1983, when Alexander Solzhenitsyn, the Russian
writer and dissident, received the Templeton Prize for
Progress in Religion, he began his acceptance speech by
saying:

Over half a century ago, while I was still a child, I recall hearing a number of older people offer the following explanation for the great disasters that had befallen Russia. "People have forgotten God — that's why all this has happened." And if I were called upon to identify briefly the principle trait of the entire twentieth century hereto, I would be unable to find anything more precise than to repeat once again, "People have forgotten God."

Our children need to know that, behind all life — the giraffe, the dinosaur, the stars, a cob of corn — there is this Who, this Personal Creator, who puts something of the divine nature into everyone of us and gives life value, meaning, and sacredness. When we believe this truth, it holds some powerful implications for us.

The first implication is this — if we believe that the cause of existence is a person that we can come to know, then we live in a personalized world. In this we are like children, because one of the ways a child makes sense of its life and surroundings is to personalize everything. When we are young, we talk about Mr. Sun, and we give names to our dolls and teddy bears. I remember, as a child, seeing houses and trees and automobiles all having faces. Not all were smiling! But they formed, nonetheless, my personal world. Everything was a Who. As we grow older, however, the Who becomes a What and How Much.

Dr. Seuss's Christmas classic, *How the Grinch Stole Christmas*, is a story about a community called Whoville. The residents are an incurably happy people with a secret that the Grinch cannot understand. So, when he tries to steal Christmas from Whoville, he takes the trees, the turkey, the presents, and the cake. But the Whos, stripped of all this, go ahead and celebrate Christmas anyway. Although the Grinch eventually capitulates and joins the citizens of Whoville at their party, the secret of their happiness is left up to the reader to discover.

Maybe their secret has everything to do with the fact that they were Whos — not Whats or How Muches or How Bigs. Their very "whoness" is what was sacred. The Grinch could not steal the fact that people and relationships are what counts, that the sacredness of life lies in who we are, who loves us, and who made us.

The second implication of the truth of a Personal Creator is that we don't live in this world alone. It is not a world just for me, for the self — we have neighbours. God has created us to be part of a community.

Surely one of the central themes or ideas of the creation story is the intimate inter-relationship between every part of God's creation. There is a pattern, a plan, and a purpose to everything. Humankind is certainly seen as the crown of creation. But we live in a vital, responsible, and accountable relationship with all created things because, like us, they have purpose and sacredness. We recognize this fact explicitly when we perform a Blessing of the Animals. And we know it implicitly, because everything we make or do affects somehow the environment around us.

Did you know that on most beds there are about two million microscopic dust mites, most of them alive? I'm not sure who actually counted them, but it is estimated that ten per cent of the weight of a pillow is dust mites. None of us sleeps alone! Chapter one of Genesis describes a world with all its parts living in harmony. From Genesis, and from our own experience, we know that it *does* matter if we clear a mountainside of its trees, just as it matters that people need wood and paper, work and homes. We do not live in a world separate from the dust mites or the trees, or the animals that depend on the trees. And that's one of the lessons we learn in Genesis.

The third implication of this truth is that there is only one Eden, one first home — not many. Every human has one beginning, one Creator. But our ethnic origin is not chapter one in the Book of Life — it is chapter two. Chapter one tells us of a more basic origin — a place of unity and love, not fear and hate; a place of order, not chaos; a place of beauty, not ugliness; a place of cooperation, not competition; a place of eternity, not time and death. Although that world is lost to us at present, we need to know that it can be reclaimed and we can be redeemed through Jesus Christ,

The New Testament takes great pains to identify Jesus as the Second Adam, and traces his genealogy, beyond his ethnic Jewish roots, to Adam. Many of us make chapter two of Genesis the starting point of our journey, forgetting (or perhaps not knowing) about chapter one. In the first chapter, Africans and Arabs, Aboriginals and Asians, even Europeans, all began as two people — Eve and Adam. And God said, "It is very good."

The first great question that we ask, you'll recall, is Who? The second question is Why. Why did God do all this? Why did God make the earth, the stars, the sun, and me? The answer comes from another text, a newer text, the Gospel of John. He explains, "For God so loved the world that he gave his only Son, so that everyone who believes in him may not perish but may have eternal life" (John 3:16). And even when the world became broken, and the love became fear and the order became chaos, God still loved and gave us the possibility of Eden restored.

I want my children, my grandchildren, and their children to know who really made them. I want them to know that they live in a Whoville — not a Whatville or a How Muchville. I want them also to know that in their life story there is a "chapter one" that tells them they are united in a common humanity, where all persons are made of one blood and created in the image of God.

I want them to know that all are sacred and all are loved, that the dream of a perfect God-centred world is part of our memory, that God put it there, and that in Christ it can be redeemed and rediscovered. If our children, and their children, are going to know these things, they have to know the story and we have to tell them, so that they and we together can sing, "All things bright and beautiful, all creatures great and small, all things wise and wonderful, the Lord God made them all."

Father of all life, renew in me the memory that values the Who more than the How Much, the memory that makes sacred all living things, that speaks of one home, one beginning for all peoples, and one love that has the power to redeem all our waste and selfishness, through Jesus Christ our Lord. Amen.

The
Eden Affair

The man and his wife heard the sound of the Lord God walking in the garden at the time of the evening breeze, and they hid themselves from the presence of the Lord God among the trees of the garden. But the Lord God called to the man, "Where are you?"

(Genesis 3: 8 – 9)

One of the very humbling realities of the nineties is our confusion about how to deal with new forms of evil and violence in our society. This is humbling, because we somehow thought science and education would so modify human behaviour that social peace and harmony would be the logical result. Not so! In spite of the efforts of social workers and educators, crime and its consequences leave us with more questions than answers.

We read stories of children killing one another or killing their parents, often without any appearance of remorse or conscience. We ask Why, and no one answers. Were we not promised "all things bright and beautiful?" Did we not hear somewhere that universal day care, universal health care, and universal education would bring a return to paradise? Why then the disappointment? What have we missed?

What we've missed is one of the key Bible stories about the choices we make and the friends we keep, and living with the consequences of both. I'm calling it the "Eden affair." It is the story of a perfect place where all of life is lived in absolute harmony, where everything works. But then something happens. The garden called Eden becomes a place of fear and shame. Communication fails, relationships break down, murder is committed, and paradise is lost.

When we read our newspapers and watch our television news, we hear all about what's wrong. It's about national disunity, debt and unemployment, lawlessness and crime, poverty and homelessness. These are pressing issues in our country, and we feel it's wrong that they exist. We ask Why? If God really made a perfect world, and if God is God, then what went wrong? Why the hurt?

Although we point the blame at our leaders and our systems, at big business and organized religion, some of us want to go past that, to be more personal, more vulnerable. We want to ask not what's wrong with government or our justice system, but what's wrong with people? And what's wrong, perhaps, with me? Why do I hurt? And why do I hurt others? These are the real questions we need to ask.

The story begins in a garden. The Greek word for garden is paradise. God has made it. Into it come a man and a woman — Adam and Eve. They are created partners with God and each other. Unlike other animals in the garden, Adam and Eve are aware of themselves. They know their names. They can reason and make decisions, and they can create. They are given a sense of awe and respect, appreciation and responsibility, for all they see in the garden. They are also given the gift of relationships — with God and one another. They can sense the other — the needs of the other, a love for the other. This love is above instinct and simple attraction. It is a love that sees their relationship grow.

They are also given another relationship, a relationship with God. God clearly doesn't want Adam and Eve to be like puppets on strings. God wants to be their friend and gives them the gift of choice, the right to say Yes or No. This is a risk that God takes because of love. As a sign and symbol of this relationship, God plants in the midst of the garden a tree, the tree of the knowledge of good and evil.

This, God says, is a special place, a sacred place. And the tree is a constant reminder that, in order to make the world work, "we need to be friends." The tree says two things. First, it says that God loves Adam and Eve. Secondly, it says that they need to love and trust God. By saying No to the fruit of the tree, we say Yes to God.

Eve and Adam enjoy this arrangement for a time and

thrive by it, until one day a new being shows up and introduces itself. Although we call it serpent or snake, the Hebrew word can be translated Shining One; so let's just say it was a Dazzler. In the dialogue that follows, the Dazzler zeroes in on this sacred tree. In essence, the Dazzler offers Eve (and I'm sure Adam wasn't far behind) some new ideas about their relationship with the tree and, therefore, with God. As Genesis says, "The serpent was crafty." It asks a series of questions. "Did God say that you weren't to eat the fruit of this tree?" In other words, the Dazzler suggests, "Did God say No to you? How can a father who loves you ever say No?" Well, Eve listened to that, as you and I listen.

The second statement of the Dazzler is, "If you do eat the apples, I happen to know that you won't die. As a matter of fact, quite the opposite. You'll have both your eyes and thoughts expanded to wild possibilities. And if I could go on," says the Dazzler, "when you eat those apples from that sacred tree, you won't need God anymore. You'll be your own God. This garden will all belong to you."

Well, it's a familiar old story. But it's as if it happened yesterday. And in fact, it keeps happening. It's what the drug dealer says to the child on the playground. It's what a man or woman says to a business partner when they want to make some easy money. It's what we all say when we want something we shouldn't have but take it anyway. Eve looked at the tree and saw that it was "good for food, a delight to the eyes, and could make her wise." She called Adam over to the tree. They had lunch, and for the first time forgot to thank God. And their lives changed. They felt a new heaviness inside them. There was a sense of disharmony and dislocation. Everything looked different.

Then, as evening came, they heard a voice, the voice of an old friend; and they hid themselves. God called out, "Where are you, I've lost track." And they said, "We were afraid and we hid, and we are ashamed. We violated the tree, that sacred place." Then they began to blame each other. "It's not my fault. It's hers." And Eve said, "It was the Dazzler." The result is that Eden was lost, and consequently life is infected by a kind of virus that makes us ashamed of who we are. We are afraid and uncertain where our true home is. And we are helpless to retrieve what we once had.

There are several important things we need to hear from this story — things that are essential for a happy life. The first is that, in the centre of our lives, there grows something sacred, something that speaks of goodness and mercy and hope, something that is not under our control. We need to reverence it and obey it, in order to live. The Eden story speaks clearly of our need to have, at the centre of everyday life, this something that speaks to us of the sacred reality beyond the self, a Personal Reality to Whom I am accountable and with Whom I am in relationship.

A few years ago in an issue of *Atlantic Monthly,* there was a political science article by Glenn Tinder, entitled "Can We Be Good Without God?" Dr. Scott Peck, responding to this question in his book, *A World Waiting to be Born,* says, "Yes . . when the living is easy." When it's not, our best self and best values are never enough. The truth is that, without a relationship with God at the centre of our world, life does not work as it was intended. All other relationships eventually loose their sacredness, and we become like Adam and Eve — afraid, alone, ashamed, and hiding from what used to be good.

The second important aspect of this story is that it

contains the greatest lie ever told — namely, that we don't need God at the centre of our lives, that we can get along better on our own, and that any deity that says No to you is not worth keeping. The Eden affair tells us that evil is introduced into the human situation when men and women — and children — believe this lie. Evil comes into the world because people choose it over the good.

Dr. Scott Peck, in another of his books, *People of the Lie,* writes, "There are only two states of being: submission to God and goodness or the refusal to submit to anything beyond one's own will — which refusal automatically enslaves one to the forces of evil." Or as C. S. Lewis put it in *Christianity and Culture,* "There is no neutral ground in the universe: every square inch, every split second is claimed by God and counter-claimed by Satan."

The third important principle in this story is that our happiness and success is partly dependent on the choices we make. We are the product of our choices. Like Adam and Eve, we live with the consequences. There is one positive choice that any of us can make at any point in our lives. It is a redemptive choice. It is a choice that is offered on every page of the Bible from Genesis to Revelation. It is a choice that reclaims the essence of Eden.

Probably the best form of the choice comes in the invitation written in Matthew's gospel. "Come to me all you who are weary and are carrying heavy burdens and I will give you rest. Take my yoke upon you and you will learn from me and you will find rest for your souls. For my yoke is easy and my burden is light." Jesus of Nazareth says, "Follow me." Saying Yes to that offer begins the process of putting the sacred centre back where it belongs. It is the first choice we make in reclaiming Eden.

Finally, the story leaves us with two questions. They are found in the text. They are timeless questions for every generation, for ours and our children's. Both questions come from God. They are addressed first to Adam and Eve and then to their child. The questions are first, "Where are you?" (Genesis 3: 9), and secondly, "Where is your brother?" (Genesis 4: 9). These questions arise from of a sense of alienation, lostness, and broken relationships. But also, and more important, they come from a God who wants to transcend all of that, who longs to know us, to love us as children, and to see us love one another.

How will we answer? Adam and Eve answered by saying, "We were afraid, and we hid because we were ashamed and naked." Cain, their son, answered, "I don't know where my brother is. Am I my brother's keeper?" Good questions, but not good answers. We know where the good answers can be found, but we have to choose to find them. This is why the Eden affair is one of the stories we need to know.

Holy God, we hear your voice in the garden, calling us to be friends, but we hide from you. We would sooner take the apples than know you as the centre of life. Renew in us a deep need to adore your gifts, not just to consume them, so that, when the enemy tempts us with the lie, we can turn to you without shame or fear, and find your fulfilling grace, through Jesus Christ our Lord. Amen.

The
Rainbow Connection

Noah found favour in the sight of the Lord . . . Noah was a righteous man, blameless in his generation; Noah walked with God.

(Genesis 6:8 – 9)

This is the story of a man, a very old man — so old that he lived "before the flood." After Adam and Eve disobeyed God in the garden of Eden, their lives — and human history generally — went from bad to worse. It was as if Hell's Angels and Satan's Choice had taken over the world. "The Lord saw that the wickedness of human kind was great in the earth, and that every inclination of the thoughts of their hearts was only evil, continually. And the Lord was sorry that he had made humankind on the earth, and it grieved him to his heart" (Genesis 6:5).

God, who had intended all life to be good and responsible and at peace with itself, looked at creation and was deeply hurt. God wanted to start over. Evil was everywhere; it had infected all of life. And God acted. First, God chose the family of a man named Noah. The scriptures say that Noah was a righteous man and that God told Noah of his plan. "The earth is corrupt, filled with violence, all life contaminated in its ways. I have determined to make an end of it and to start again." And God gives Noah the blueprints for a great ark, a floating barn, 450 feet long and 75 feet wide, to be made of gopherwood. So, to the astonishment of his neighbours, Noah set about building the ark.

God told Noah not to worry about what his neighbours might think. God said to Noah, "You will be my new beginning. Take two of every living creature and fill the ark with life. You've got just about a week! In seven days it's going to rain for forty days and forty nights, but you will be safe in the ark."

And that's the way it happened. The flood came, and all of life outside the ark was destroyed, and the ark floated for one hundred and fifty days. Near the end of that time, Noah looked for a sign of hope, some indication that he and his ark would soon reach dry land. So he sent out one of his ravens, and then a dove. When the dove came back with an olive branch in its beak, Noah knew it had discovered life. When he sent the dove out again and it did not return, Noah knew it had found a home.

Soon the water receded, the ark touched land, and life began again. But then God told Noah how life had changed. The surprise is not that human nature had altered, but that God's nature had changed. God had developed a new strategy. Instead of retribution, God opted for relationship. "I am establishing my covenant with you. There are no conditions. I want to be partners with you. Never — never again — will I destroy all that I have made. As a sign, I will hang up my bow, never to be used again as a weapon but rather as a promise, a promise that I am your partner and friend." And God put a rainbow in the clouds and said to Noah, "This is the sign of the covenant that I make between me and you and every living creature that is with you, for all future generations" (Genesis 9:13).

It's a wonderful story. It has all the ingredients for an Andrew Lloyd Webber production. It's a story we need to hear again. The tale of Noah's ark raises many issues that we face today — violence, death, destruction; looking for signs of hope, beginning again; asking the question, Do we have a second chance? The story is relevant today because some of us are afraid that "it's raining again." By this I mean that the times are scary. We are afraid for our own safety and the safety of our children. People are doing crazy things, nations are tearing themselves apart, and we are afraid. From that fear comes depression, and from depression, anger.

I visited a school in Toronto last year. Just inside the main door was an art display, put together by students in the senior grades. It was a very impressive showing and,

I'm sure, deserved high marks. But somehow I found it disturbing. The themes that dominated the work were fear, anger, destruction, and violence. There was little sign of gentleness, kindness, freedom, or hope. There was more death than life. And because genuine art reveals the soul of the artist, I am worried. These works say plainly that our children are afraid. But is it any wonder? We live in the world of the nineties — a world of downsizing, ozone depletion, cutbacks, ethnic cleansing, less money for education, fewer opportunities for employment. Maybe we have good reason to think that it's raining again.

Many of us, like Noah, may feel that we believe and worship and pray alone. We come to church, but we're often the only people on our street that do. We feel, even in our religion, isolated and afraid. We start looking for a place to hide, a place of shelter, a place of salvation. I see a lot of people looking for some ark of safety. They don't say that, of course. They call it, "looking for something more," for meaning or mystery. They sense that it has started to rain again. And the first thing we need to know from this old story is that the rain is going to stop, pain and fear do not last forever, the bad guys don't win. That's what the rainbow means. It's about hope. God is ultimately in control.

One of the most courageous women I know of is Lesley Parrott, who lives in Toronto. In 1986 her daughter, Allison, was murdered. The crime has never been solved. She has written about her feelings in order to help others. She acknowledges that, although many people have supported her and been kind to her, none has been able to take the pain away. Yet she would say that, because of a warm Christian upbringing, she has been able to recognize and accept and embrace goodness when she needed it. In the April 1993 issue of the United Church *Observer*, she writes, "I believe we cannot wait till tragedy strikes to reach out and show that the power of love is more pervasive than the power of evil. Let's make sure that love, caring, and joy are so strong that, when we confront evil, we are able to survive and emerge as victors."

Someone has written that hope works in these ways — it looks for the good in people instead of harping on the worst; it discovers what can be done instead of grumbling about what cannot; it regards problems, large or small, as opportunities; it pushes ahead when it would be easy to quit; it lights a candle instead of cursing the darkness. It is important to realize that the only people in the Noah story who could hope were in the ark! Consequently, we need to tell our children where to find the ark — where they can go to be safe and hear about new beginnings, second chances, and goodness winning over evil.

Where do our children go to find the rainbow? Many of us see our homes and families as arks — places of protection, security, and direction. But there is another ark — we call it the Church. We're not talking about the building or the institution, but the spiritual Church, which we sense whenever and wherever God's people gather. When that happens, we experience the redeeming love of Christ, the good news of the cross of Christ, and the hope and encouragement that come from the knowledge of Christ.

Yes, we know there are some major leaks in this old ark. Yes, sometimes we're not sure where we're going or who's in charge. Yet it is in this place, with these people, where so many of us have come in out of the rain and found a reason to begin again. It is a place where we have heard a voice and sensed a grace that has told us how God will give us a second chance. There is life after the flood. The Church is a place of hope, and we're there whenever two or three are gathered, whenever we bow our heads with our friends and families and give thanks, whenever we pause alone and reflect upon Whose we are. We're in the ark whenever we take our children for a walk through the fall leaves and tell them who made those leaves and who, after the winter, will make them again. Yes, we have an ark. Our children need to know where that is.

The most important thing about the Noah story is what we learn about God himself. Certainly, the most powerful words in the story are "never again." "Never again," God says, "will I destroy the land. I will not hurt you like this again." As we saw earlier, a dramatic change happens in this story. It is not so much that human nature alters, but that God changes. God does not seek retaliation and retribution, but is committed to relationship and redemption. He says to Noah, "This is the sign of the covenant that I make with you. Never again will I destroy the earth. When the rainbow is in the clouds, I will remember my promise" (Genesis 9:16).

God has continued to remember, and God's promise stands — even when the world said No to his commandments and built a golden calf instead; even when we refused to listen to his prophets; even when we met God's son and heard him and said, "Crucify him." God, hiding the tears, remembered his covenant and took his sword and planted it in the earth, a sword that became a cross. He says to us, "Never again! I will keep loving you. I will keep suffering with you. I will keep forgiving you."

The final thing we need to hear from this story is a good word about Noah. Children often ask, "What do we do when it's raining?" In other words, how do I get through these hard, difficult times? Noah lived in terrible times but, the Bible says, "He was faithful and took God at his word, and he kept building the ark."

I am reminded of a story that the actor Charleton Heston tells about the filming of the great epic movie *Ben Hur.* Heston found out in the course of the production that he was to be in a great chariot race. He went to director Cecil B. de Mille and told him frankly that he was not comfortable with horses. He said that he had never ridden a chariot. He didn't know how. The great director responded and said, "Let's take a week. You learn to drive the chariot. We'll put the production on hold until you do." A week later Heston came back and said, "Well, I've learned to drive the chariot, and I've adjusted to the horses, but I'm not very good. I'll never win the race." De Mille's great words were, "You stay in the race. I'll see to it that you win."

I hear God saying to us, "Stay in the race. Stick with the ark. Keep sending out the dove. And some day you will see my rainbow saying to you, 'Never again, never again!' I'll see to it that you win."

God of hope, who looks for friendship instead of retribution, we call to you out of the flood of our violent and fearful world. Renew in us the assurance of your faithfulness, energy, and will to build a place where you are honoured; and give us faith to stay in the race, through Jesus Christ our Lord. Amen.

The Bush that Talked

The angel of the Lord appeared to Moses in a flame of fire out of a bush; he looked, and the bush was blazing, yet it was not consumed. Then Moses said, "I must turn aside and look at this great sight."

(Exodus 3: 2 – 3)

Sometimes, on a midwinter Saturday afternoon, I like to "channel surf" in search of golf. I like to see all that lovely green grass, the trees in full leaf, and people in T-shirts and shorts. Once while I was skimming through the channels, I happened to hit on Vision TV (a channel for religious programming in Canada). There, speaking to me with conviction and some strength, was a young woman in her thirties who turned out to be a spokesperson for the Sikh religion. She was addressing a conference for Sikh Canadian youth, pleading with them to retain their faith. She spoke of the moral values taught by the elders — symbolized by the turban, the dagger, and the bracelets. She said, "We must be strong; otherwise we will be swallowed up by Western values that can offer us only pornography, greed, drugs, and the breakdown of the family." I kept listening, stunned but impressed by her critique. In her message, I was hearing echoes of Charles Colson, Mother Teresa, and Alexander Solzhenitsyn, all of whom have been saying the same things and issuing the same warnings.

This leads to the question, How is it that many of the loudest voices of Western culture are voices of alienation, perversion, greed, and rights without responsibility? Where are the voices that speak to our children of the true virtues of the Christian faith, which is supposedly one of the foundations of Western culture? Who speaks to them of self-discipline, responsibility, honesty, compassion, and faith? Where do we go to hear the clear voice that tells us who we are, how to live, what is right, where is hope?

In her very unique way, Annie Dillard, the American short-story writer, speaks to this problem in her book, *Teaching a Stone to Talk.* "Nature's silence is its one remark . . . We as a people have moved from pantheism to pan-atheism. Silence is not our heritage but our destiny." Then she goes on to say, "We have doused the burning bush and cannot rekindle it; we are lighting matches in vain under every green tree." Is it possible that in Western culture we've tried to douse the burning bush, douse the voice of God?

The story of Moses and the burning bush is found in chapter three of Exodus. It is the story of a man just minding his own business in the wilderness outback. But then God calls him, gets his attention, and speaks to him. The burning bush has come to be a powerful symbol for what we call "revealed religion" — that is, religion that comes directly from the divine source above, rather than from the process of human thought and reflection. Revealed religion holds that we did not think up God, but instead, that God thought of us, and also revealed the divine nature to us.

Revealed religion, therefore, is not something that evolves; it is "handed down" from God directly. These statements from God, written in stone — if you like — do not change. They are as relevant and applicable now as they were in 1400 B.C. or A.D. 30. So when Dillard says, "We have doused the burning bush," she means that Western culture — whose values were rooted in the revealed faith of Judaism and Christianity — is trying to drown out those ancient voices. We have ceased to listen. Instead of heeding the burning bush, we are content to light our own wet matches under things that will never burn and never give us spiritual light or warmth.

Every one of us will be much poorer if the bush that talked is silenced. We will be missing seven eternal truths about God, truths revealed in that chapter of Exodus. To extend the metaphor, we might call them the seven branches of the burning bush.

The first branch is God calling out, "Moses, Moses" (Exodus 3:4). Here is a God who knows us and calls us by name. God initiates the relationship with us. The last thing Moses was looking for was God or religion. He was hiding. He had gone to the outback of the desert, running away from responsibility. But God found him. God is not dealing primarily with a people, a crowd, or a classroom. God begins with a person. William James has said that God makes a private visit with the individual. That's the way God works.

The second branch is God's admonition, "Come no closer, remove the sandals from your feet, for the place on which you are standing is holy ground" (Exodus 3:5). This tells us that God is a holy God — above us, not of this world, but Spirit. So, while being personal, God still puts this significant distance between humanity and divinity, a distance we might call sacred space. This is the reason we instinctively worship on our knees.

The third branch is God's statement, "I am the God of your father, the God of Abraham, the God of Isaac, and the God of Jacob" (Exodus 3:6). In short, God has given us our very history. God knows who we are and where we've come from — better than we know ourselves. As Psalm 139 says, "Lord, you have searched me out and known me; you know my sitting down and my rising up; you discern my thoughts from afar." God knows our past and accepts us in spite of it.

The fourth branch is God's assertion, "I have observed the misery of my people who are in Egypt. Indeed, I know their sufferings" (Exodus 3:7). He is a God who sees our pain, who has compassion for those of us who suffer.

The fifth branch is God's promise, "I will deliver you and my people, and take you to a new land flowing with milk and honey" (Exodus 3:8). Here we see a God of hope and promise, a God who not only sees our pain but who responds to it. As Jeremiah has written, "For I know the plans that I have for you, plans for goodness, not calamity. To give you a future and a hope" (Jeremiah 29:11). The poet Emily Dickinson has written, "'Hope' is the thing with feathers — that perches in the soul — and sings the tune without the words — and never stops — at all."

The sixth branch is God's statement, "So Moses, I will send you" (Exodus 3:10). Here is a God who not only calls us by name and sees our pain, but also calls us to get off our knees and be a partner in the divine healing process. God works with people and speaks through them. God says to Moses, "Here is a return ticket to Egypt. You will speak for me before Pharaoh, that he would let my people go. Some day you will come and worship me on this mountain." So God calls us to be partners in liberation. The English author and mystic, Evelyn Underhill, once wrote that Christ wants not nibblers of the possible but grabbers of the impossible.

The seventh branch is God's promise, "I will be with you" (Exodus 3:12). He is the God of grace, the God of comfort, the God of support, the God who enables us to do what he calls us to do. Moses says, "But God, you're expecting too much. Who am I? Why would pharaoh ever listen to me?" And God just says, "I will be with you. I am the God who knows your name, who knows your history, who sees your suffering, who promises freedom and deliverance. I ask you to trust me, and I will be with you."

What do we miss when we dismiss such stories as archaic fantasies and myths, when we walk away proud of our independence, when we douse this mystical and sacred bush with the water of our arrogance and self-importance? What are the implications for us if we do that?

First, we rob ourselves and our culture of the sense of the sacred mystery. There can be nothing ultimately sacred without Someone Sacred making it so. We cannot do that ourselves. God, revealed in scripture, has declared that human life is sacred, that family is sacred, that sex is sacred, that our human commitments to one another are sacred. When you invite God to leave the sacred place, life becomes shallow and hollow.

It is a great contradiction that Canadians still say we are a God-loving nation. In spite of the fact that church-going continues to decline below twenty per cent, eighty per cent of us told *Maclean's* magazine in the spring of 1992 that we believed in God, even Jesus. Yet the desecration of things sacred continues. Perhaps we have just retired God, put him on the bench, given him the gold watch, and declared him God Emeritus.

The second implication of dousing the burning bush is that we rob ourselves of the chance to hear the voice, the word that comes out of the eternal silence, that tells us who we are, how to live, why to live, what is right, and where is hope. The voice of God calls all of us and each of us by name. God says to us, "I made you. I see your pain, and I promise you a future and a hope. I will never leave you."

The third implication of dousing the bush is that we miss God's message of liberation. We miss the word that says there is someone who can redeem our lives, who sees the bondage, sees our helplessness, and has the power and the will to deliver us and set us free. Here is a God who says, "Let my people go." He is the same God who "loved us so much that he gave his only son as the lamb that takes away the sins of the world. That whoever believes in him will not perish, but will have everlasting life" (John 3:16). Is not this the voice that comes out of the ancient story, the voice that we need to hear? And not only us, but our children and grandchildren need to hear this voice.

It is time for us to stop trying insanely to douse the bush. Instead we need to put it where it belongs, in the centre of our lives — to humbly draw close to it, recognize its sacredness, take off the shoes from our feet, and simply sit and listen and obey. Where else can we hear a voice that calls us by name, that recognizes our pain, that promises us deliverance and hope?

O God of love, who calls us by name and sees our pain, renew in us the joy of your redeeming action. May we see again the hope of people made free, of nations reborn. Give us the courage to go, to speak, and to act for you, through Jesus Christ our Lord. Amen.

New Rules for a Better World

God spoke all these words: I am the Lord your God, who brought you out of the land of Egypt, out of the house of slavery. You shall have no other gods before me . . . Moses said to the people, "Do not be afraid; for God has come only to test you and to put the fear of him upon you so that you do not sin."

(Exodus 20:1 – 2, 20)

Our news media now bring us accounts of violent acts such as most of us cannot remember hearing before. In the Gaspé coast town of Ste. Anne des Monts, student violence and defiance of teachers closed down the secondary school for several days in the fall of 1993. That same year in Atikokan, Ontario, a 15-year-old student held a teacher and another student at gunpoint in a classroom dispute over mustard being spilt on his clothes. Sexual abuse cases involving trusted people in authority continue to scandalize our institutions and communities. Cases of family violence fill our courts, and we all ask Why? What is happening? What is this strange virus that seems to be sweeping through the structures of our society creating this climate of fear, suspicion, and anger?

We are used to hearing and reading about violence that takes place somewhere else, not in our own backyard. Canada's armed forces have been deployed in the cause of peace-keeping for many years, always responding to situations where civil order has broken down, where the rules of proper behaviour have been violated, where nations who promised peace have used that promise as a pretence for violence and aggression against their neighbours. When the rules are broken and violence results, the cost to nations, tribes, families, neighbourhoods, and marriages is very high.

Many of us can remember that, after the Second World War, there was a universal passion for lasting peace. Out of that yearning the United Nations was born. The United Nations developed a charter of new rules to protect the sovereignty of every nation. Since then, hundreds of new laws protecting ethnic minorities, human rights, and the rights of children have been promulgated. All of us have benefitted from these laws. Yet, considering the horrific incidents we read about in our newspapers, will any number of laws be enough to counter this virus of anger and violence?

Every time new problems hit the public scene, the cry is immediate. We need a new law. We need more gun control. We need to revise the Young Offenders' Act. We cry to the government, the courts, and the police, "Please solve our problem. Pass a new law. Build more prisons. Give police better guns." But I'm afraid that what's causing our current malaise defies all the rules. New prisons, more police, and all the laws that parliament can pass won't stop a 15-year-old from arming himself in the classroom. Such behaviour is born in a deeper place — a troubled heart.

Columnist Michael Valpy, writing in the 3 November 1993 issue of *The Globe and Mail* under the heading, "The Troubled Children of Families of Convenience," quotes Dr. Paul Steinhauer of the Hospital for Sick Children in Toronto. "The lives of increasing numbers of young Canadians are foundering because of two crucial but inadequately met biological and social needs — the need for a satisfactory and continuous attachment to a parental figure, and the need to tame and diffuse inherent human aggression."

In other words, too many of the youth in our nation are missing the consistent parental love, trust, and discipline that will nurture self-esteem, and build self-control and respect for others. There are social conventions that tell us how we should live. There are rules instructing us to respect, honour, and obey. There are rules against spouse abuse. There are rules telling those in positions of power to respect the weak and the helpless. There are rules that give every child the right to be loved, protected, and nurtured during the formative years of its life. But all these rules are broken or ignored.

One of the key Bible stories is about rules. It starts with a tribe of very confused and frightened people. For generations they had been slaves, workers without dignity or rights. They had forgotten who they were. Life was mere survival. But one day, liberation came. It came with a promise of freedom, a new home, and a prophecy that they would some day be a great nation. Their leader was Moses. The God of these people had appeared to Moses, calling him to new leadership. After this confused and dysfunctional tribe was safe on the east side of the Red Sea, Moses began the task of building a nation out of them, a nation whose people would have a distinctive relationship with God and with each other.

Moses begins by receiving from God a set of laws. These laws would make his people strong, give them dignity and identity. These laws, if obeyed, would actually bring harmony and peace. The history of this people is interesting. Whenever they live by the laws, they prosper. Whenever they forget and go their own way, the nation begins to come apart.

I remember a labour negotiator, who worked for the federal government some years ago, saying that Moses was the first great labour negotiator of all time. He was the one who settled things between God and Israel. When Moses had finished his work on Mount Sinai and had received the ten commandments from God, he came down from the mountain and gave a news conference. He said, "This agreement has good news and bad news. The good news is that I've got God down to only ten commandments. The bad news is that adultery is still in."

It would be interesting to hear what we all think about the ten commandments. To some of us, perhaps, they are out of date — too heavy, too negative, too much guilt, too many thou-shalt-nots. In the 10 September 1990 issue of *Christianity Today,* Ted Turner, the newspaper and cable giant, is quoted as saying, "We should dispense with the outmoded and irrelevant Ten Commandments altogether. I bet nobody here even pays much attention to'em, because they are too old." Instead he says we need Ten Voluntary Initiatives that include helping the down-trodden, loving planet Earth, and limiting families to two children. I'm not sure that voluntary initiatives solve our problem. Loving one's children is not voluntary. Being faithful in a marriage is not voluntary. Respecting human life is not voluntary. Keeping our word is not voluntary. To really thrive, children need, first of all, a sustained relationship with a parent and, second, restrained behaviour through rules and discipline.

This is exactly what we have in the Ten Commandments. They begin with the words, "I am the Lord your God, who brought you out of the land of Egypt, out of the house of slavery" (Exodus 20:2). It is the voice of a loving parent saying, "I am the one who has given you freedom. I am the one who has given you a nation. I created you. I love you and I have great plans for you. I make my covenant with you and promise that I will be in relationship with you forever." Before saying, "Thou shalt not," God first says, "I shall."

The only parent who has the right to ask her children to obey her is the one who first says Yes to them. The only teacher that has the right to be obeyed, is the one who is committed to the education and well being of every student in his classroom. Morality that works is born not in laws passed by parliament, but in a relationship that creates a climate of trust and mutual respect. It is a law written nowhere else but in the human heart. That is where God begins. It is an ethic born of grace. God always says Yes before saying No.

The first four commandments deal with how to maintain this primary relationship with God. They tell us who to worship, how to worship, and when to worship. They are rules designed to protect the sacred covenant between God and us. There can be no moral system that works without accountability to someone other than the self. As Fyodor Dostoyevsky said, "When there is no God, everything is permitted."

The rest of the commandments deal with other relationships and other things we need to value, to live in civil harmony with each other. They deal with commitment to family, commitment to marriage, commitment to the value of human life, commitment to respect for our neighbour and our neighbour's property, integrity, and household. Could this be the law we are looking for, a law not written on the walls of classrooms or even churches but written in our hearts.

The American sociologist, Robert Bellah, in his book, *Habits of the Heart,* has written, "Perhaps life is not a race whose only goal is being foremost. Perhaps enduring commitment to those we love and civil friendship towards our fellow citizens are preferable to restless competition and anxious self-defence. Perhaps common worship, in which we express our gratitude and wonder in the face of the mystery of being itself, is the most important thing of all. If so, we will have to change our lives and begin to remember what we have been happier to forget."

What do we do with all of this? Why is this story one of those great stories we need to know? Jesus tells a different story of two houses, both having the same builder, the same design, the same number of bathrooms and fireplaces, and both with a two-car garage. One day it started to rain. The wind started to blow and there was a great storm. When the storm passed and the sun came out again, one of those homes had disappeared. It was the one built on sand. The house that survived, however, was built on rock.

What each of us needs to hear from this story is that we need to check our foundations. We need to check our basements and find out what laws are written on the walls. Are we morally, spiritually, and socially living on something solid, something built on God; or is it something only of our own making and, therefore, built on sand? We need to know because, we are afraid, the storm has come. It is a storm of violence and dysfunction and tragedy, and we hear about it every day through the media.

Jesus said, "Love the Lord your God, with all your heart, soul, mind, and strength, and love your neighbour as yourself" (Luke 10:27). Our response needs to be, "Lord, have mercy upon us, and write both these thy laws in our hearts, we beseech thee."

It's hard to read the papers, Lord. Children are killing one another, sometimes killing their parents. We seem to be drifting into more confusion and violence. It's hard to understand. Renew in us, Lord, a love of your law. Give us a new will to say No to the wrong and Yes to responsibility and service, through Jesus Christ our Lord. Amen.

Five Smooth Stones

David said, "The Lord who saved me from the paw of the lion and from the paw of the bear, will save me from this Philistine" . . . Then he took his staff in his hand, and chose five smooth stones . . . his sling was in hand, and he drew near to the Philistine.

(1 Samuel 17: 37, 40)

When the Toronto Blue Jays won the World Series for the second time, thousands of people in Toronto crowded Yonge Street for a victory parade. The next day, through the intimacy of television, we got a closer look at our heroes in the Skydome. All of them were out of uniform. We heard them talk, and we saw a little more of the kind of people they really are. Television is such a probing, invasive thing. Close-up facial expressions, even chewing and spitting, are displayed for our evaluation. Yes, they are heroes. And yes, they are champions. But also, they are every-day kind of guys.

Television does the same with any leader — Church leaders or political leaders. Sometimes it gets almost too close, and we see things we would rather not see. But indeed, these are our leaders and heroes, warts and all.

One of the important festivals of Church life is the celebration of All Saints. This is when the Church asks us to pause and focus on a different kind of champion and a different kind of victory. These people have fought the good fight of faith, have persevered and endured. They have been victorious not just until the playoffs next year or the election in four years, but for life. When we celebrate All Saints' Day, we celebrate the heroes of the Spirit, the heroes of the faith.

There are many women and men, throughout history, whose biblical names we recognize — Noah, Abraham, Sarah, Moses, David, Mary, John, Paul, and Peter, to name just a few. It is very interesting how the Bible treats its heroes. None of them is portrayed as a saint. In these marvellous scripture stories, the writers, like the television camera, get up close; and we see some very flawed people, people who knew failure and fear yet were chosen to do great things for God. In the words of Oscar Wilde, "Every saint has a past, and every sinner has a future."

Such are the life and times of King David, son of Jesse, hero of Israel, champion over the Philistines, father of Solomon, and writer of the psalms. It is the classic story of the little guy who makes good. God tells Samuel, the prophet, to go to Bethlehem, to a family fathered by Jesse. Jesse had a number of sons. One of them, God tells the prophet, will be king over Israel. Samuel does the usual thing. He looks for the strongest, brightest, and most mature. "Not so," says God, "Do not look at his appearance or the height of his stature, for the Lord looks on the heart" (1 Samuel 16:7).

When Samuel meets David — the youngest, smallest, and weakest — God says, "This is the one. Anoint him," and the Spirit of the Lord came mightily upon David. The life of David is a story with many chapters. Like many of us, he has victories and failures. There are times of joy and times of shame. There are the classic stories of his triumph over Goliath, his victory over the armies of Saul, his conquest of Jerusalem. And then, at the peak of his power, he abuses it, forgetting his accountability to Someone Higher.

David sees the woman, Bathsheba, bathing. In his lust for her, he breaks all the rules, including the commandments against adultery and killing. First he has sex with Bathsheba and makes her pregnant; then he arranges for the death of her husband, Uriah, in battle. This was truly a fatal attraction. After the death of her husband, Bathsheba moves in with David and becomes his wife. David thinks that no one sees, but the scripture tells us, "The thing that David had done displeased the Lord." Nathan, the prophet, confronts David with the truth. David confesses and repents, and God forgives him. Then David says to Nathan, "I have sinned against the Lord." And Nathan replies, "The Lord has put away your sin;

you shall not die" (2 Samuel 12:1, 13).

David's life is very much a mix of conflict and victory, of despair and hope. His family becomes probably the most dysfunctional one in the Bible, but David retains a powerful and profound spirituality, out of which he writes the psalms. A paraphrase of Psalm 30 reads, "I said I am so strong, I never shall be moved. But You, Lord, shook my life, my heart was in distress. I cried out for your help and pleaded for your grace."

Probably the most loved and popular of all the stories of David, is the story of David and Goliath. The people of Israel are threatened by a powerful and brutal enemy, the Philistines, who have a hero, Goliath. He is over seven feet tall, three hundred pounds, and all muscle. He loudly defies any of the Israelites to meet him, one on one, winner take all. Saul, the king of Israel, is afraid, fearing that Goliath surely will defeat any of his warriors.

David, young and very confident, says to the king, "Let me take on Goliath." Saul says, "But you are only a boy." David replies, "The Lord who saved me from the paw of the lion and the paw of the bear, will save me from the hand of this Philistine" (1 Samuel 17:37). So, without armour or sword, David steps up and takes on Goliath. Picking up, for his slingshot, five smooth stones from a little stream, he moves toward Goliath. After some heated words with Goliath, David runs toward him. Circling the sling above his head, David lets go a stone at close range, and hits Goliath in the forehead with such power that the giant topples over and dies. The Philistines, without a leader, run. And David, the little guy from Bethlehem, is a hero.

The reasons why our children need to know this story are two. First, very simply, all of us have Goliaths in our lives. There are things, situations, pressures, people who seem stronger than we are. Like brick walls, they stand there, defying us to take them on. Too often we are reduced to helplessness and weakness. Second, we need to know how David did what he did. What was the source of his strength? Where did it come from? Was it just ego and nerve? Or was it something else?

The scripture says that David picked up five smooth stones. I'm not sure why he did that. He only used one! I think, at the very least, they are symbolic of five things that David had going for him, that made him immensely strong in the face of his enemy. They are the same five smooth stones that we can use to give us the strong edge against any Philistine, whether that is fear or grief.

The first stone is *knowing Whose we are* and, therefore, who we are. David was God's anointed, and he knew it. When you and I truly believe that we are children of God, born out of the image and love of God, and never alone, that will make us strong. In his book, *Wishful Thinking,* Frederick Buechner says, "A Christian is one who points at Christ and says, 'I can't prove a thing, but there's something about his eyes and his voice. There's something about the way he carries his head, his hands, the way he carries his cross — the way he carries me.'" When we know Whose we are and Who carries us, we are strong.

The second stone is *being who we are* and not trying to be someone else. We need to use just what we have been given. David was offered armour and sword, but they weren't for him. They were five sizes too big. He was a shepherd. That's the way he met Goliath. Albert Schweitzer, in the February 1969 issue of *Pulpit Magazine,* is quoted as saying, "A man can do only what he can do. But if he does that each day, he can sleep at night and do it again the next day." There is power in being just who we are.

The third stone is *knowing that you are doing the right thing.* It is the power of conviction. Knowing the truth and letting it set you free doesn't mean being politically correct or doing the expedient thing. David knew right was on his side. The bully was wrong. God's people could not be laughed at too long. He acted.

The fourth stone is *knowing the source of your power.* David said, "The Lord has saved me from the paw of the lion and the paw of the bear. He will save me from the hand of this Philistine" (1 Samuel 17:37). It does make a difference when we acknowledge that the energy that makes things right in our lives comes from Someone Higher and Other than ourselves. Sometimes we need to say that out loud. Knowing the source of our power makes us strong.

The fifth stone is *the will to act,* the inner strength that we control, that puts one foot in front of the other. It is our refusal to be the victim any longer. "The sling was in his hand and he drew near to the Philistine."

These are five smooth stones. At first sight, they seem insignificant against such a foe. But David would tell us that any one of them can slay most Philistines.

Some of us may recall the name of Joyce Milgaard. She is the mother of David Milgaard, who was released after serving twenty-three years in prison for a murder he claims he did not commit. Joyce Milgaard is a woman who discovered and used those five smooth stones. Out of her love for her son and her strong faith in God, she fought to have her son released. She was successful because (1) she knew Whose she was; (2) she acted out of who she was, a mother; (3) she believed firmly in the innocence of her son against many odds, and she knew she was doing the right thing; (4) she knew where her power came from; (5) she had the will to act and persist in that action.

The 27 April 1992 issue of *Maclean's* magazine contains these words: "In Joyce Milgaard's alert, direct gaze, there is a hint of the resolve that enabled her to persevere with what often seemed to be a lost cause." She credits Christian faith with giving her the strength to pursue her goal. She took great solace from the fact that, every day, God forgave her mistakes and enabled her to start anew. "I have a deep faith in God. His law supersedes other laws. If we follow Him, we come out winners." Then, in the same article, *Maclean's* comments, "The image of Milgaard that emerges from her successful battle is, fittingly, a biblical one — David versus Goliath. The judicial establishment is big, but Joyce Milgaard has the sling." It's a great story about a courageous women, a woman who knew the power of five small smooth stones.

People ask us, "Does faith in God, and a relationship with Jesus Christ, make any difference when you have to face the giant alone?" I know what Joyce Milgaard would say. I know what King David would say. I know what all the saints would say. "I worship you, O Lord, for you have raised me up; I cried to you for help, and you restored my soul. You brought me back from death, and saved me from the grave" (Psalm 30:1–3 in *Psalm Praise*).

Lord, stand with us when the giants come. Renew in us a sense of Whose we are and who we are. Give us true values, a knowledge of what is just and right, dependence on your power, and a new will to step forward in courage, through Jesus Christ our Lord. Amen.

Coming in Second and Loving It

John testified to him and cried out, "This was he, of whom I said, 'He who comes after me ranks ahead of me.' I am not worthy to untie the thong of his sandal."

(John 1:15, 27)

There is something in all of us that longs to be first. It begins, perhaps, when we are children — part of an original blessing or original sin, I'm not sure which. We play our games to win. We run our races to win. Often this burden rests most heavily on the firstborn in a family. Expectations are high, and the feeling of responsibility to succeed is high. All of us like to tell about family members who come in first.

Some years ago at Christmas, my wife and I decided, for the first time, to compose one of the those Christmas form letters. It was a letter of information about our past year, written chiefly for friends and family whom we seldom see. We were feeling pretty good about this work of Christmas cheer, until we read an article in *The Globe and Mail.* "How nice — computer-generated laundry lists of other families' super-human achievements can make a dark, raw, winter day even worse." We quickly gave our letter a proof-reading against excessive positive achievement, wondering how honest we needed to be about the balance between success and failure.

We love to talk about opportunities, but seldom about conflict. Most of us struggle, on some level, with the guilt of non-achievement, but others seem obsessed with being first. It takes over their lives. We all know people, even in the best circles, who have a real need to come first. There are others who sit in our prisons, because they were willing to risk everything — they got it, but then lost it. We remember the tragic stories of athletes Tonya Harding and Ben Johnson, who wanted not just to be good but the best, to be first at all costs. We all lose when our leaders are like that. We all lose when blind ambition becomes god.

In his book, *Both My Houses,* former Member of Parliament, Sean O'Sullivan, talks about political ambition, particularly his own. He considers the temptation to be at the top — how it can blind a person to the true value of other people, and destroy the very thing that good politics are meant to achieve. O'Sullivan, who died of leukaemia, spent the last part of his life as a priest. In his later years, still as a young man, he tried very much to seek reconciliation with old foes, rather than pursue the race that brings loneliness and bitterness.

The story of John the Baptist is about a man who found his greatness by coming in second. The writer of the gospel story described not so much who John was, but who he was not. We read verses like, "He himself was not the light." "I am not the Messiah." "I am not worthy to untie the thong of his sandal" (John 1:20, 27). The deeds of John the Baptist reveals a man who was anything but a shrinking violet. Standing in the wilderness alone, calling people to change their lives and repent and be baptised, telling the religious establishment that they were a family of snakes leading the people of God down the garden path. Here was a man who took a back seat to no one.

John lived in an age when people could remember those who sought messiahship. They were religious leaders, charismatic personalities who had collected followers but faded into history. John was probably head and shoulders above any of them — he had integrity, the ability to attract disciples, a message which was strong and powerful. Obviously there was a movement around John, saying, "Yes, he is the Messiah; he is the anointed one of God. Follow him." It would have been very tempting for John to believe it, but he does not. He says, "I am just the voice, crying in the wilderness, preparing the way of the Lord. There comes One after me, who is greater than I." John is an amazing leader who comes in second and loves it.

We live in a culture that finds it hard to understand people like that. We wonder about people who are content to take second place, to let someone else go ahead in the line. Current values in Western culture don't leave much room for such people. We want to be first. We push our children to be first. Somehow we've equated first with best. We live in times when people crave leadership. We elect candidates to positions above us; then, before the paint in their office is dry, we begin to criticize and throw stones. Sometimes it's only too obvious why we do that. All of us really want to be leaders. All of us really want to be in charge. Not that we want the responsibility, not that we're going to be good at it, but just because we want to be first.

You may have heard the story of how many preachers it takes to change a light bulb. The answer is ten — one to get up on the chair and change the bulb, nine others to say, "I could have done better."

In many books and articles that I read about spirituality, I find a phenomenal spiritual hunger. I see people creating their own spirituality and their own religion. The significant point about most of these "home-made" religions is that they make God a peer, or at best, a big brother or uncle. In this situation, the believer, not the believed, becomes the authority.

For many years, scholars have been writing books about Jesus. This trend perhaps began with Albert Schweitzer's search for the historical Jesus. A contemporary example is A. N. Wilson's book, titled simply *Jesus*. To me, the Jesus that emerges from the last chapters of many of these books seems very anaemic and weak, unsure of who he is, desperately in need of psychotherapy. In other words, we lower our image of Jesus, so that we might control him. John the Baptist says, "That's not what it's about. I am not, but he is. He is a man who ranks ahead of me, because he was before me. He is the Lamb of God."

Some time ago, I was a guest at a sports celebrity banquet. Sitting at the head table were members of the elite club of winners in both amateur and professional sport. They had come in first and done themselves, and us, proud. After breakfast, there was an address by a sports announcer from New York. One of the points he made was about leadership; and because everyone in the room was a leader, both in business and industry, we listened. Central to his message was that every good leader needs first to be a follower. No great athletes get to the top without good coaches that they admire, obey, and imitate.

I hear John the Baptist saying to us that — as individuals, as families, as a church, and as a society — "we are not ourselves by ourselves." We become our best only when there is someone other whom we admire, obey, and imitate. We become leaders by first being followers of someone who has been at the top. It is what the writer of the psalms meant when he said, "I would rather be one that holds the door in the house of God, than to sit at the head table in the tents of the ungodly."

All of us have heard the term "secular society," which simply means a society or a nation that has no spiritual or religious foundation. In a secular society, God is simply not an issue. Eugene Peterson, writing in the 8 November 1993 issue of *Christianity Today* says, "A secular culture is a culture reduced to *thing* and *function* . . . We North Americans have been doing this for well over a century . . . And we all seem to be surprised that this magnificent achievement of secularism — all these things! all these activities! — has produced an epidemic of loneliness and boredom. We are surprised to find ourselves lonely behind the wheel of a BMW or bored nearly to death as we advance from one prestigious job to another." The problem is that secularism marginalizes and eventually obliterates the two essentials of human fullness — intimacy and transcendence.

Intimacy is the experience of human love, trust, and joy, while transcendence is the experience of divine love, trust, and joy. These experiences do not come from more things, more freedom, and more activities. They are the gift of Someone Other. They come when we follow. They come when we put ourselves second to the One who says, "I am come that you might have life, and have it more abundantly."

We see the consequences of secularism best at Christmas time when, for so many people, the celebration is about things and activities. We spend more money every year because, frankly, it's the only thing we know to do. All of it, however, is a fraudulent substitute for the real values — intimacy and transcendence, love of friends and family, love from God who visited the earth in Christ. Real Christmas comes only when we acknowledge that we can't be ourselves by ourselves. We need to humble ourselves and come in second. It seems to me that the one human activity that accomplishes this for us is worship. It's why we set aside church buildings and call them sacred. These are places where you lower your voice, bow your head, take off your hat, bend the knee, keep silence.

Every time we do that from the heart, we have a friend beside us who whispers, "I am not that Light, and neither are you. I am not the Messiah, and neither are you. Then, he points us to Someone else, and says, "There goes the Lamb of God — follow him, admire him, obey him, imitate him; for he is the Light, he is the Messiah, he is first.

I am second, and being second makes me free."

Lord, deliver us from the curse of unhealthy competition, the feeling that rankles when we are not always in front of others. Teach us that we cannot be fully ourselves by ourselves, and that only in submission to you can we reach our full potential, through Jesus Christ our Lord. Amen.

Finding the Way In, by Putting Ourselves Out

Then the righteous will answer him, "Lord, when was it that
we saw you hungry and gave you food, or thirsty and gave you
something to drink? . . . And the king will answer them, "Truly
I tell you, just as you did it to one of the least of these who are
members of my family, you did it to me."

(Matthew 25:37, 40)

Some time ago, my sister and I were having lunch with my father, and the three of us were reminiscing about our childhood, which was a very happy time for us. We were reminding Dad of the stories he used to tell while he put us to bed. One of my earliest memories was of a woman, a friend of my parents. She was a widow who used to babysit us when my parents were away, and she always arrived with a book of stories. The stories she told us, and the stories I told my children when they were young, were designed to put them to sleep, to calm their fears, and to reassure them that someone was in charge.

Probably the most significant thing about bedtime stories is that they provide an occasion for parents to spend time with their children. The television is turned off, and it's "quiet time." The family is together. The peace and comfort of bedtime stories remind me of a wonderful painting hanging in my study at home. Jesus is sitting on a bench and listening to a little child. She is telling him a story in an animated fashion, and he is looking at her and listening with great intent. I imagine that, when she is finished, Jesus thanks her and invites her to sit on the bench with him, because he has a story to tell her.

Among the stories our children need to hear, many of them come from the Bible. The best Bible stories tell of the highest hope, the greatest joy, the deepest and longest-lasting love that anyone can know. One of the best reasons for parents to bring their children to baptism is to introduce them to Biblical storytelling. Not only baptism, but life in the Church in general, invites your child and you into a circle, into a family, where you can come in and sit down and listen to stories. These stories talk about Whose you are, who you are, Who made you, and Who loves you. They tell us of the real value, not only of ourselves but of our sisters and brothers, and how we need to get along with them.

There are many stories about a special friend, the man called Jesus, who is often not only the story teller but himself the story. The biblical story, the Christian story, has many chapters, and we all have our favourites. When I was putting this series together, I had to include not just stories we like to hear, but also stories we *need* to hear. This section deals with one of the stories we need to hear.

I have a vivid memory of watching a television interview with the late Senator Robert Kennedy. The interview took place on a train as he was campaigning in the midwest. At first the questions centred on politics. Then they turned to his children. "Above all," he said, "I want them to make a contribution. I don't care where they make it; I don't care who sees them. I just want them to make a difference in the lives of people."

I remember that interview, because what Kennedy wanted is so different from what many of us, as parents, want for our children. All of us have high expectations for them — that means a good education with good marks leading to knowing the right people, getting the right job, and of course, earning a good income. We want security for them. But is there more?

Along with the familiar stories that Jesus told, there is another parable that we need to hear. It's about being where we *don't* want to be. It's about people that we would rather *not* notice. It's about *giving* when we would rather be taking. It's about *loving* when we would rather be loved. It's about taking risks when we would rather be secure. It's a story that tells where the highest joy of human existence can be found.

A friend of mine returned from Haiti recently. Because

of the political strife there, Canadians were asked to leave. She had been working in a school in downtown Port au Prince. If she were with us today, she would probably tell us that those last few years had been the happiest time of her life. We would want to ask Why? Was it because of security, a great income, cool tropical breezes? Certainly it would be none of these.

In the gospel of Matthew, as Jesus is finishing his teaching ministry, he tells a story about accountability, about judgement. It is also a story about where we can find him. Jesus is to be found in some very strange places, and he calls us to join him there. "Just before I leave," he says, "I want to tell you where you can find me. Yes, I'll be in church, I'll be in the Bible, I'll be in your Bible study group. Yes, I'll be in the sacrament of the Eucharist. But also, I'm going to be somewhere else. You will find me in the food bank, the shelter, the nursing home, the prison."

Someday, Jesus says, he will gather all peoples, and on that day there will be two kinds of people — some disappointed and some happily surprised. Those who are surprised will hear words like these: "When I was hungry and thirsty, you fed me. When I was a stranger, you took me in. When I was in rags, you clothed me. When I was sick, you took care of me. When I was in prison, you visited me." They will say, "Where, Lord, did we see you, hungry and naked?" Jesus will say to them, "What you did for the least of my friends, you did for me" (Matthew 25:35).

The vital importance of this story is that it takes many of our money- and pleasure-based values and turns them absolutely on their head. Many symbols remind us of the presence of Christ — the cross, the Bible, the candle. But this story adds one more — the towel, the sign of service.

Ruth Harms Calkin, in her book, *Tell Me Again, Lord, I Forget,* writes this poem.

> You know, Lord, how I serve you
> with great emotional fervour in the limelight.
> You know how eagerly I speak for You at the
> Women's Club.
> You know my genuine enthusiasm at a Bible
> Study,
> But how would I react, I wonder,
> if you pointed to a basin of water
> and asked me to wash the calloused feet
> of a bent and wrinkled old woman
> day after day, month after month,
> in a room where nobody saw and nobody knew?

All of us would find that very hard. We do not come to service easily, but when we do, Christ promises us to be already there. He puts his arm around us and welcomes us. Eugene Kennedy, in his book, *Free to Be Human,* writes, "Bighearted people have learned to give up something of themselves, in order to make room for other people in their lives. There is no loving — no generous giving — except by those who have been willing to face down their own selfishness and try to pry open the grasping hand that would close only on their own concerns."

In his book, *The Body,* Charles Colson tells the story of his visit to a prison for women in Raleigh, North Carolina. It was Christmas Day 1985, and he spoke at a service for two hundred inmates. As he was getting ready to leave, the prison chaplain asked if he would visit Bessie Shipp. "Who is Bessie Shipp?" he asked. "Bessie has AIDS," said the chaplain. "She's in an isolation cell. It's Christmas and no body has visited her." Less was known about AIDS in 1985, and Colson confesses that he hesitated and was somewhat afraid. He said quickly, "I'm running late for the men's prison." But he buried his fear and went with the chaplain. "As the chaplain escorted me through two secured areas, he explained that ... the doctors had given her only a few weeks to live. A chill came over me."

Colson writes that, as he entered the cell, he saw a petite young woman sitting bundled in a bathrobe and reading the Bible. She looked up. Her eyes brightened as the chaplain said, "I promised I'd bring you a Christmas present, Bessie." After the pleasantries, Colson asked if she had yet found Jesus in her book. She said that she had been looking for the Christmas story but didn't know where to find it. He opened the book and read the story to her, and the conversation continued. They prayed together. Tears flowed that morning. It was a life-changing moment for Bessie, and for Colson.

Two days later she was released, and a week after that, baptized in a local church. The people in the church took her in and cared for her. Three weeks after that, Bessie died. It was a Christmas Charles Colson can never forget. "I was in prison," Jesus said, "and you visited me."

Certainly one of the great paradoxes and mysteries of life is that we find ourselves by losing ourselves. We find the way to joy, to great love, to deep fulfilment, when we put ourselves out for other people, especially those in need. This is a message we all need to hear. We watch television and see human suffering, but we see it at a distance. We need to know that this is not just tragedy but opportunity for service, a service that leads not only to something for self but to something for others. It is part of our search for God and for the presence of God's spirit.

We do need to look in all the "right" places for God. We will find God in worship and prayer and small fellowships. But we will also find God with the friends of God, those people in great need. They include the hungry, the sick, the lonely, and those in prison. If our children and grandchildren are to grow up as balanced people, they will need to know that human suffering is not just a problem out there to watch, but a problem they can do something about. This last parable of Jesus may not be our favourite bedtime story, but it is certainly one our children need to know.

Lord, help us to face down our own selfishness and give up our own space and time, to make room for those who hurt and those who are alone. Yes, it will cost us something. May we find your joy in paying that price, through Jesus Christ our Lord. Amen.

The Tragedy
of Unforgiveness

Peter came and said to him, "Lord, if another member of the
church sins against me, how often should I forgive? As many
as seven times?" Jesus said to him, "Not seven times, but, I
tell you, seventy-seven times."

(Matthew 18:21, 22)

I remember hearing a story of a young couple who were engaged to be married. It was wartime, 1943. He was a soldier; she was a teacher. Almost overnight, his unit was moved to the Pacific. There was no time to marry, just promises and farewell. At first she got frequent letters and wrote replies immediately. After about six months, his letters stopped coming. The War Department wasn't sure where he was, and declared him "missing in action." During the next year, there was no word. She was lonely, teaching in a small town. She met someone. The relationship became intimate, but only for a brief time.

A month later, she received word that her fiancé had been taken prisoner, had been released, and was now coming home. She was delighted and remembered, very much, her love for him. Soon after his arrival home, they were married. All seemed well, until one day he said, "It must have been hard to be faithful to me, when I was away." Her response was not what he had expected. She paused, "There's something I should tell you." Out came the story with much regret. She said, "I'm so sorry, Peter, can you forgive me?" It took Peter awhile, but he said he did.

But strangely, in the months and even years that followed, whenever Peter would say, "Good night" or "I'm going out," he would often add, "And, remember Ann, I forgive you." It became, at least, a weekly occurrence. One night when Ann was in the kitchen, he said again, "Ann, thanks for dinner and just remember, I forgive you." There was no response from Ann this time, only the sound of the screen door closing behind her. Without a kind of forgiveness that is more than words, that is from the heart, it is hard to have a relationship. Many of us have great difficulty forgiving those who have trespassed against us. In an article entitled "Holocaust and Ethnic Cleansing" in the 16 August 1993 issue of *Christianity Today*, Philip

Yancy, refering to atrocities in the Balkans, notes the price the world pays for the "terrible logic of unforgiveness." Those responsible for violence have not been able to forget or forgive hurt inflicted in the past. Yancy quotes essayist, Lance Morrow: "Where unforgiveness reigns, a Newtonian law comes into play: For every atrocity, there must be an equal and opposite atrocity."

The story of unforgiveness is not unique to the Balkans. It is the story of many nations. It is the story of families, of any one of us who have been wronged and want what we call "justice," which is sometimes only retribution. We don't have to look far for the results of unforgiveness. Read the great tragedies of Shakespeare, *Macbeth* and *Richard III*. Read Francis Coppola's *Godfather I, II, and III.* See Clint Eastwood's film which won the Academy Award for best picture, *Unforgiven.*

The question here is not whether we should forgive those who have wronged us. Most of us know we should. We remember the words well: "Forgive us our wrongs, as we forgive those who have wronged us." The serious issue is how we can reverse the cycle of unforgiveness. How can I — in a situation where hurt and damage stands between me and someone I care about — find reason to forgive? Such forgiveness is more than words; it is from the heart; it heals the relationship. How do we teach our children — in their relationships with friends, brothers and sisters, and us — to forgive and not to hold grudges? It is possible that learning to forgive is something like learning a language. It begins in childhood, but it needs to be taught and reinforced over and over again.

One of the stories we need to know is written in chapter 18 of Matthew's gospel. It is a story about forgiveness and unforgiveness. A man refuses to forgive his friend and, as a result, upsets many of his other friends. They know that he has just been forgiven a great debt that he could never have repaid. The key message in this parable of Jesus is that we have a reason to forgive — we have already been forgiven. Because we fail to grasp the reality that we are a forgiven people, we find it difficult to forgive others. This is also the reason why many of us find it difficult to forgive ourselves.

The problem with the man in the story is that he had missed the experience of forgiveness altogether. He thought that he had simply "got off the hook" for a debt that was equivalent to millions of dollars. It never crossed his mind that he was being forgiven from the heart by someone who clearly understood the enormity of his debt. That someone was willing to let it go, stop keeping score, and throw away the file. With the debt out of the way, the barrier was removed, and they could get to know one another again.

But when the forgiven debtor went back to his neighbourhood, he found a friend that owed him $50. He insisted on repayment. The friend pleaded with him, as he himself had pleaded. But the man who had been forgiven refused to forgive this small debt, and we know the rest of the story. Because he refused to forgive the $50 debt, the authorities threw the debtor into prison. In her book, *The Seeds of Heaven,* Barbara Brown Taylor writes, "The wicked servant was *already* behind bars, bars of his own making. By refusing to be forgiven and refusing to forgive, he had already created his own little Alcatraz, where he sat in solitary confinement with his calculator and kept track of his accounts."

The best reason that you and I have for forgiving, is that we have been forgiven ourselves, by a God who knows us better than anyone. This God knows that the warranty on our self-righteousness has run out long ago, and that we stand in great debt. Yet this same God, through love for us, has read our file, torn it up, and thrown it away. God went to the cross for us. The blood of Christ was shed for us, so that we might be totally forgiven. God in Christ saw our debt and forgave us.

There is a story I like, told by a priest who was serving in the Philippines. He was pestered by a woman who told him that she spoke with Jesus every day, and that he told her things that only he knew. The priest was sceptical of this Philippine piety, and was cool towards the woman. But she kept pestering him. Finally he told her that the next time she was talking with Jesus, she was to ask him about an incident that occurred when the priest was young, an incident that had caused him much guilt. "Ask Jesus to tell you that story," he said. A short time later, the woman was in church again. The priest asked her, "Did you talk to Jesus this week?" "Oh yes," she said, "I did. He spoke well of you, Father. But about the incident —he told me that he had completely forgotten." When someone like Jesus stops keeping score on you, you feel rather foolish keeping score on other people.

Several years ago, I was called home from my holidays to comfort and support a family. The daughter, while driving impaired the wrong way on a one-way street, had caused the deaths of two young men. I did not know the victims or their families, but only this young woman who had made a terrible mistake. She was guilty. She was in great remorse. She was worried about the families and, justifiably, the legal consequences. I happened to be with her family on the morning of the funeral of one of the victims. The girl's parents were going to attend. Just before they left, the phone rang.

It was the mother of the victim. She identified herself and said, "We are about to go to church to attend the funeral. We will be receiving Holy Communion. Would you tell your daughter that we forgive her?" You have no idea the difference that phone call made to those people — and to their guilt oppressed daughter. Although she still had to face a possible jail sentence, someone — the only person who could — had given her a second chance.

This is the message in Jesus' parable of the debtor. This is why we need to tell our children the story. There is Someone beyond ourselves who knows us, who loves us, who recognizes everything that we have done, and yet forgives us. Our children need to know that, when they feel guilty, they are not alone with the guilt. There is One who has died for them, to cover the cost of their mistakes and their wrongs. They need to know that and, as a result, have hope.

Jesus said to Peter, "It is not just seven times that you forgive, but seventy times seven." He was simply saying, "You can't keep score any more, because the world for you is now different. The warranty on your goodness has run out. But God, through love for you, forgives you anyway." We, God's people, are called to do that for others — to do what God has done for us.

Lord, we hurt easily and let it happen. We don't do much about it. We let friendships go because it hurts too much to bear the pain. Renew in us a love for people that refuses to give them up, a love like Yours, that bears all things, believes all things, forgives all things, simply because it's the way You love us, through Jesus Christ our Lord. Amen.

The God
Who Runs to Meet Us

So he set off and went to his father. But while he was still far off, his father saw him and was filled with compassion; he ran and put his arms around him and kissed him.

(Luke 15:20)

In a community not far away, three old friends, just past retirement, used to get together about ten o'clock in the morning for coffee and doughnuts in their local Tim Horton's. They talked about everything, including politics, religion, and the weather. Sometimes they discussed their children. Two of them were married, one was a widower, all of them had children. Often they would compare notes, brag, complain, or share frustrations. They were honest with each other. It was a Friday morning in April, just after Easter. Charlie was a little late. It gave George and Sam time to order the coffee and get into their first doughnut.

Charlie arrived a little out of breath and looked a little tired. But he had this big smile on his face. George nudged Sam, "Charlie, heavy date last night?" "Well, you'll never guess what happened," said Charlie, "David came home." There was silence from his friends, a very uncomfortable silence. "But, Charlie, you thought he was dead." (George knew he was treading on very sensitive ground.) "Yes, I did," said Charlie. "You haven't heard from him in two years. You were so good to that boy, Charlie, you gave him everything. He just took it and left. It's been two years. He's never called you. I would have written him off long ago." "Let's have some more coffee," said Sam.

"Fellas," said Charlie, "it may sound crazy, but last night was the best night of my life. I thought he was dead, you see. I saw him coming up the driveway. He had changed a little, but it certainly was him. I froze. In that split second, I thought of his mother (he looks like her, you know). I ran to him and we hugged." "Well," said George (remembering the conversations about David over the past two years), "I hope you told him about the pain he's caused you. Hope you told him how wrong he's been, using you like that. It makes me boil just thinking about it."

"Well actually, we threw a party," said Charlie, "Couldn't help myself. I dressed David up in my best suit, gave him his grandfather's ring, gave him a pair of Rockports, got a twenty pound roast of beef, prime rib. We had a party! He's my child. I thought he was dead. I thought he was lost, but he's come home. He told me he was sorry. He wants to start again. I have to try, fellas. I invited him for coffee. Hope that's okay."

There is a story much like this told by Jesus in chapter 15 of the gospel of Luke. It is probably *the* most important story our children need to know. Like many of the parables of Jesus, it is a timeless and powerful story, because it touches us where many of us "live." Some of us, as parents, identify with the Father. We know about the cost of loving our children, and the painful struggle between justice and compassion.

Others of us, recalling former days, identify with the wayward son. We remember those crazy times in our lives when we woke up in that "far country," knowing ourselves to be lost, having feelings of self-loathing, and facing the choices needed to find our way home. Yet others of us sympathize with Charlie's coffee-time friends, recognizing the "older brother syndrome" that "makes us boil" when we hear of extravagant love being poured out on those who, we think, least deserve it.

The story speaks to us not only on the level of personal feelings and family dynamics, but also on a deeper level, the level where God deals with us. It speaks to us of those times when we pack our religious bags and say, "I'll go it alone now." We leave our heritage behind and take our own way. It speaks of the attraction of that far country. God is "out of our hair," and we do what we want, satisfying every longing and enjoying it, for awhile.

Then we reach a point where we begin to sense that we've lost more than we've found. The guilt is stronger than the joy. The memory of where we came from, and who we've left behind, begins to preoccupy our thinking. We have to make a decision about what's best for the rest of our lives. We have to decide whether we can swallow our pride and admit we blew it, change our direction and start the long journey home — the journey to what we know is right. The story speaks especially of God, who acts in this most unpredictable way, who sees us coming, has compassion, runs to meet us, embraces us, and forgives us.

The value of this story, like many others in the Bible, is that it gives us a set of unique truths wrapped in relational language. There are three important truths in this parable.

The first truth is that this parable speaks of God, and what God wants for us, in a particular way. God is not just any God. He is Father, the Father of creation. He is revealed in scripture as the One who brings all things to life and loves with an everlasting love. He gives us freedom, even the freedom to leave him. He lets us go, even to a far country. He waits for us to come back, and when we do, he forgives, accepts, and includes us. He is the God who runs to meet us.

The parable speaks of God as a loving parent who wants the best for us. Not all of us have that kind of memory of our childhood. That is why we need to have this one. Here is a Father who, when he welcomes us home, instead of dressing us in castoffs, goes into his own closet and gives us his best. It says in scripture, "Quick, bring the best" — the best robe, the best ring, the best pair of shoes. Here was the robe of dignity that reminded the son of who he was, his value, his worth — things that he had lost in the far country. Here was the family ring that spoke of where he belonged and who wanted him to be there.

The second truth is that there is, for all of us, a place called home. Again we are using human language to describe a spiritual reality. Home is the place where we are at our best — a place of dignity and worth, of ultimate security, where we truly belong, where we are accepted and unconditionally loved. God dwells in that place, and we find it when we are in relationship with God. We are free to turn our back and leave and run to a far country, but that place is always there. There is a figure standing in the doorway, waiting, ready to run to meet us.

T. S. Eliot, in his *Four Quartets,* has written,

> We shall not cease from exploration
> And the end of all our exploring
> Will be to arrive where we started
> And know the place for the first time.

It is crucial that we give our children a memory of this home. That's why we need to tell them the story of scripture. That's why we need to give them positive experiences of Church and Sunday School. It's a place that includes them, loves them, wants them; a place where they are given the best — dignity, worth, love, and values of right behaviour. Some day, when they are tired of the far country, they will have a memory of how it "might be" for them.

The third truth has to do with the term "far country." Most of us, at some point in our lives, long to escape responsibility and authority, to run from God and go it alone. And most of us actually do escape at one time or another. We indulge ourselves and love it. We have a great time. For many people that is life. They live for themselves, to themselves, and by themselves. They are at home in the far country, and they even die there.

The value of Jesus' story is this — it tells of at least one person who is not at home in the far country. After many failed relationships, loss of control over life, and guilt that has become too heavy, the person starts to think about the way life is unfolding, and finally he "comes to himself." He wonders about the future. He once thought that by living in a far country he could be his own master. But that didn't work. There must be a better way. Helmut Thielicke, in his book, *The Waiting Father,* has written, "We are always subject to one master. Either to God [or] to ourselves . . . The question we face is whether we want to be the child of the one or the slave of the other."

It could be argued that, in a secular culture like ours, all of us have left for a far country where the mandate is freedom and personal rights, loss of responsibility and suspicion of authority; where appearance and exclusivism and everything that money can buy have become central values. In such a far country, we are surprised when the community disintegrates and our streets aren't safe. We are surprised when sport has more to do with money and gambling than healthy competition. We are surprised when violence against women and the vulnerable become not just crime but entertainment that brings in millions to pornographers and their dealers. This is our far country.

Central to our purpose as a Church, is to keep alive a memory of somewhere else — a home, a place of integrity, dignity, righteousness, and community. This is where relationships are held sacred, where responsibility and authority are not bad words, where God is seen as a loving and compassionate Father waiting to run to meet us. The Church's mission is to keep that possibility and memory of home alive, so that those who are tired of the far country, who are tired of being slaves to what some call freedom "come to themselves," and opt to return home. They are people who recognize that only in a relationship with God can there be a future.

So we have this simple yet profound story, of a home where all of us really belong, and of a far country where part of us longs to be, even though being there is to live without hope. The most profound and best part of the story is that God waits for us to return. And when he sees us on our way, he runs to meet us. This too is a story we need to know and remember.

Lord, we have been in that "far country" far too long. At times we have deceived ourselves that it was home, that it was everything. Thank you for the grace that calls us to come to ourselves, confess the lies we have lived, and turn back to what we once denied, through Jesus Christ our Lord. Amen.

A Supper to Remember

The Lord Jesus, on the night when he was betrayed, took a loaf of bread, and when he had given thanks, he broke it and said, "This is my body that is for you. Do this in remembrance of me" . . . For as often as you eat this bread and drink the cup, you proclaim the Lord's death until he comes.

(1 Corinthians 11:23–24, 26)

All of us know the power of memories. The recall of past situations has the power to make us laugh, blush, feel anger or depression. Many of us live, from time to time, under the tyranny of memories — things we'd rather forget, even things we thought we'd forgotten. We see a person, hear a piece of music, look at an old photo album — and there it is again. The pain or joy can be as real as it was in the original experience.

The psychotherapeutic industry pays a lot of attention to memories. We hear about the healing of memories — the need, either by prayer or therapy, to neutralize the power of the past, of deep hurt and abuse. Increasingly, in our newspapers and periodicals, we read about the controversy over the validity of buried memories of childhood abuse recalled in adult years, and the implications of such memories, not only for the victim but for the family and the community.

Although memories can be very powerful and difficult to dismiss or deny, not all are destructive. Memories have the power to unite people, to bring a family together around some happy past event. We aid our memories by putting together photo albums, videos, or home movies. Often, when our family gets together, we recall the past and reminisce. On a recent Christmas, my sister gave me an old photo of the two of us standing in the backyard of our family home. The photo was taken sometime in the late nineteen-forties. She was about four and I was near seven. Although neither of us recalls the event, we both remember our home and what a happy place it was. The memory evokes good feelings.

Every community and nation also has its defining memories. A central activity in the Jewish community is holocaust remembrance. The American film industry keeps producing footage of the Civil War, sustaining a

memory that defines much of who Americans are. A friend
of mine, who proudly puts U.E.L (United Empire Loyal-
ist) behind his name, is part of a historical club that re-
enacts 19th-century battles, especially battles of the War
of 1812–14. In full, period military dress, with muskets
and drums, they engage their American counterparts on
summer weekends — when it's not raining. As my friend
said, "We live out the memory that tells us who we are
and who we're not."

Memories have the power not only to recreate past
events in our mind, but also to give those events reality
in the present. That reality can profoundly affect our lives;
it can tell us who we are, where we belong, and where
we're going.

Christians have a central, defining memory, one that
they have ritualized and institutionalized for almost two
thousand years. Someone has written, "While some drink
in order to forget, we Christians drink in order to remember." This event is called many things — Eucharist, Holy
Communion, Lord's Supper, Breaking of Bread, and Mass.
While it has grown in different traditions and is practised
in different ways, it has been, through the years, the central act of worship for most Christians.

However different the details, whatever the language,
the Church's worship is rooted in memory. It draws its
power and reality from memory — memory that is repre-
sented and made real. As it says in the liturgy, "Christ has
died, Christ has risen, Christ will come again." Or as St.
Paul says in our text, "For as often as you eat this bread
and drink the cup, you proclaim the Lord's death until
he comes."

There are three questions that we need to ask of this
memory. One — why is it so important and so central to
our faith as Christians? Two — what real benefit is there

for me in remembering? Three — who qualifies to benefit from the memory?

First, although I've called this story "A Meal to Remember," it is never just the meal that is remembered. The meal is, instead, a means to remembering. What we remember, what we celebrate every time we break bread and share the cup, is a weekend in the life of Jesus of Nazareth. Specifically, we remember a Friday and a Sunday morning. The memory conveys pictures of a cross standing on a hill and a stone rolled away from a grave. The pictures tell the story of God in Christ redeeming the world, overcoming evil, and assuring us of a hope beyond death.

The experience of Christians has been that, when we hold up this memory, we somehow tap into its power. This is because the memory does two things. It first points to a Friday, the day Jesus died — a day of suffering, rejection, and obvious failure; a day when it seems that the bad guys win. The memory of this day very much relates to the experience of our own pain, our own grief, our own loss of hope, our own disappointments. Here we have God not just sympathizing with our human condition, but enduring it, embracing it, feeling it, and knowing what it is like.

But the memory also points to a Sunday morning. The sun breaks through. The pain passes. What seemed to have finished is just beginning. What seemed to be failure and defeat is now victory and success. Jesus, who was dead, is alive. This memory is powerful. While it identifies with us in our weakness and lostness, in our guilt and our grief, it also draws us forward. It says, "There is a future; we can't give up. There is more to life than just Friday."

The American humourist Garrison Keillor writes in 10 January 1994 issue of *Christianity Today*, "What else will do *except* faith in such a cynical, corrupt time? When the country goes temporarily to the dogs, cats must learn to be circumspect, walk on fences, sleep in trees, and have faith that all this woofing is not the last word." This memory sustains us, encourages us, and gives us the definitive hope of our lives.

And what is the benefit of this sacred meal to us? In receiving bread and wine, what do we obtain? The post-communion prayer in the Prayer Book speaks of these "holy mysteries," this "spiritual food." Obviously, there is more to the meal than wafer and wine. There is something on a deeper and higher level — "Assuring us thereby of thy favour and goodness towards us; and that we are living members of his mystical body, which is the blessed company of all faithful people; and are also heirs through hope of thy everlasting kingdom."

All of us who are regular communicants could share a wide variety of personal experiences gained while kneeling and receiving communion. These range from the profoundly mystical to nothing at all. We bring to the table our moods, our pre-occupations, the kind of week we've had, and lots of other mental baggage. Through all of this, we need to know what we can expect at the Lord's table. The Prayer of Thanksgiving says that we receive three things.

First, we receive "the favour and goodness of God towards us." When, with an honest and needy heart we participate in this sacred meal, we are assured that God loves us the way we are and feeds us through the body and blood of Christ. God's grace and favour and goodness are focused on us through the wafer and the wine.

Secondly, we are "living members." Never do we come to the Communion table alone; we come as members of a family. We are given family food. St. Paul writes, "We, who are many, are one body, for we all partake of the one bread." We are assured that we are never alone. There is a place, a home, a family where we belong, and the Eucharist assures us of that.

Thirdly, we receive "Hope of thy everlasting kingdom." God's gift of hope, the assurance that all the "cynical woofing" around us in this strange world is never the last word. We may not know what will come, but we know Who will come. If the last word about our lives belongs to God, why do we need to fear the next moment? Yes, there is Friday. But we also have Sunday morning, resurrection, hope, and eternity.

Finally, who qualifies to come to the Lord's table? Down through the ages, the Church has had a lot of fun with this. Some of us can remember rules about being old enough, dressed right, going to confession first, being confirmed first, fasting first. Although they were meant to protect the sacredness of the sacrament, the rules have often excluded and discouraged many sincere believers. I recall, one Christmas Eve, a young man passing by the church and coming in. It was about 6:15 p.m. and we were preparing for the first service. "I haven't received Communion for so long. What are the rules? How do I hold my hands? How do I dress?" He seemed serious; so I said, "There is only one rule. You need to come hungry for God."

The Prayer Book is wonderfully clear about this. The people who qualify for Communion come in four classes. They are the tired, those needing to be loved, the lost, and the guilty. This list comes from the Comfortable Words in the Prayer Book liturgy.

First, for those who are tired, there is the promise of refreshment. Doctors tell us that the symptom they hear most often is, "I'm tired." It's a new kind of "tired." It is a product of the eighties and the nineties, a product of the "fast forward" world. Jesus says to us, "Just come."

The second group that qualifies is the unloved. "For God so loved the world, that he gave." Mother Teresa has written, "The biggest disease today is not leprosy or cancer. It's the feeling of being uncared for, unwanted — deserted and alone." Jesus said, "My Father loves you." Even wanting to believe this gets us very close.

The third class of people is the lost. "A true saying," Jesus says, "that I have come into the world to save sinners." In his parables, Jesus refers often to those who are lost, who have strayed far from God and their own true path. God makes it possible to find the way.

The fourth class is the guilty. "If any one sin, we have someone who knows the Father. He is the One who makes us right with God." Being guilty and, at the same time, being able to admit it, opens doors to God's gifts of forgiveness and inner peace.

The tired are invited simply to come. The unloved are invited to be friends with God and believe. The lost are invited to take the hand of Christ and come home. The guilty are invited only to be honest, open, and repentant.

So we gather, as Christians have done for centuries and as our children will do after us, to celebrate the memory of a Friday and a Sunday morning, the memory of someone who endured a very human suffering and death, and conquered it. This memory has great power. It must be told again and again in the context of liturgy and in the sharing of bread and wine, to assure us that we have a future in God's great kingdom. Those who most appreciate it, and grow because of it, are those of us who can be honest about our need and come before God saying, "I'm tired; refresh me. I'm alone; love me. I'm lost; bring me home. I'm guilty; forgive me." It is a supper to remember. It is a story our children need to know.

Lord, we come to your table with empty hands,
celebrating not what we have done, but what you
have done for us. We are the tired; we are the lost. You
are the One who refreshes and the One who finds.
Meet us in this place, feed us with the bread of life,
Through Jesus Christ our Lord. Amen.

Reclaiming the Canadian Soul

Why do you wonder at this . . . the Author of Life . . . his name itself has made this man strong . . . the faith that is through Jesus has given him this perfect health.

(Acts 3:12, 15,16)

Among the many stories coming out of Russia following the dissolution of the Soviet Union, one involves an intriguing incident from Zagorsk, north of Moscow. Here, in one of Russia's many prisons, the governor realized that, as winter approached, he would not be able to feed his inmates even one meal a day. There was just no money left in the budget. Out of desperation, the governor went to a nearby monastery and asked the monks for help, thinking they might have food to share with the inmates. Not being used to the state asking the Church for favours, the prior of the Orthodox community took a little time but, after a few days, responded with a proposal. The monks would provide one meal a day for the next year for each inmate if the governor would let them build a chapel for the inmates in the centre of the prison.

After a long breath, the governor agreed, and a new relationship between human need and religious response began that day to transform the atmosphere in the prison. Obviously this is a story filled with irony. The state system that had rejected religion as the "opiate of the people," and turned churches into museums, was beginning to see a source of survival and hope in that very faith.

There is a story in the Acts of the Apostles about assumptions regarding the relationship between religion and a needy society, and how those assumptions should be changed. It is a story with three parts.

The first part takes place on the steps of the Temple in Jerusalem in A.D. 33. It is a busy place. Every day, at about 9:00 o'clock in the morning, a family brings their paraplegic son to sit by the main door and beg. His meagre takings may constitute the family income. Some people are generous, some not. Some get tired of seeing him and hearing his call for spare change. But the family knows that religious people have a conscience, usually a lot of guilt, and it is the "best place in town to be."

This part of the story is important, because it shows us what is too often the relationship between organized religion and the culture around it. The handicapped man is the soul of our culture — he is us. He knows what he needs and that his life is incomplete; so he searches. He tells everyone who will listen what he thinks he needs, but he never actually goes into the temple. He remains outside, claiming the crumbs that the institution and its adherents deign to offer.

As many as seventy percent of Canadians have that relationship with organized religion. We get to the steps, but not much further. From the Church we expect compassion, moral leadership, Christmas, and Easter. We expect rites of passage — baptisms, weddings, and funerals. The Church provides these and, honestly, does quite a good job. But it all happens on the steps, as far as people's hearts are concerned, and people assume that it's all the Church has to offer. So, like the man on the steps, we continue to be disabled and settle for the crumbs, and we never go any further.

This first part of the story is also a strong comment on organized religion. The Temple perhaps stands as a sign of a tired Church that willingly dispenses high festivals and rites of passage, but seldom invites those searching, those needing more, to come inside and taste the essence of it all. Perhaps the Church is no longer sure of what the essence is! So there are two losers — an institution losing an opportunity to be what it could be; and a needy person who settles for less, for the crumbs, thinking that there's nothing else.

The second part of the story is similar to the first, except that two men approach the Temple steps. They walk by with some expectancy and determination. The beggar sees this and calls out for money. The two men are Peter and John, apostles of Jesus of Nazareth. They are leaders of a new branch of Judaism called Christianity. They have seen Jesus alive after his death, they have received the Holy Spirit, and now are on fire with hope and confidence. Peter is the one who responds to the request. He says, "Look at us, we have no money, we have no crumbs to offer you. But what we have is this." And instead of giving the man money, he offers his hand and says, "In the name of Jesus, take my hand and stand up and walk — after all, isn't that what you really want?"

This story has relevance for us. It could describe a new relationship between the successful churches of our own age and the society in which they exist. This kind of Church will not only survive the last years of 20th century; it will prosper into the 21st and help a disabled society rebuild itself along the way. Such a Church will not be satisfied simply with dispensing rites of passage. Rather, it will enable and empower people, allowing them to fulfil their God-given potential, and equipping them to stand on their own two feet, to leave behind what disables and victimizes them. Such a Church will go beyond the superficial. It will invite people past the margins to the essence, past the steps through the door, and introduce them to the person of Jesus Christ.

Peter Drucker in his book, *Managing the Non-Profit Organization,* says this: "The 'non-profit' institution neither supplies goods or services nor controls. Its 'product' is neither a pair of shoes nor an effective regulation. Its product is a *changed human being.*" For a hospital, it is a cured patient. For a school, it is a child that learns and grows into a self-respecting, responsible adult. For a Church, it is people at any age who, through a relationship with Christ, discover their profound worth, the worth of their neighbour, and a hope that enables them to live responsible lives. If we in the Church are not in the business of human change, we will soon be "out of business."

The third part of the story was where we actually started. As events unfold, a crowd is attracted. The people see a former paraplegic walking, running, and jumping. He is a new man. They ask, "How has this happened?" In turn Peter asks them, "Why are you surprised?" He says, "This is what God can do, the very God that you professed to worship but in essence rejected by rejecting his Son. You killed the Author of Life, but God raised him from the dead. It is by faith in Jesus that this man has been made strong" (Acts 3:15, 16). The crowd of people were being shown that the essential element of human change is not some new invention, but something they had been offered before and had rejected. The very thing that had the power to rebuild what was broken, crippled, and coming apart, they had thrown away.

We are the crowd in the story, the crowd that once had values and virtues and a vision of possibility. And like the crowd in the Bible story, we rejected those values, those virtues, and those possibilities that God, through Christ, had offered us. Harvard President, Derek Bok, once said that during most of the twentieth century, first artists, then intellectuals, then broader segments of society, including educators, challenged every convention, every prohibition, every regulation that cramped the human spirit or blocked its appetites and ambitions.

We are the crowd that has rejected the spiritual source of those values and virtues that have been the foundation of any goodness or righteousness experienced by Western society. We have settled for the crumbs, the rites of passage, which too often have been devoid of any lasting spiritual or moral significance. We are the crowd who, in the 1990s, are watching the level of violence get out of control in our schools, on the streets, and in homes and restaurants. And like the crowd in the story, we ask Why? Some of us call for more police, others for gun control, and still others for more prisons. But this preacher from the first century, Peter, simply says, "Why are you surprised? You have rejected the Author of Life, and now you are reaping the product of that rejection."

In the 7 March 1994 issue of *Christianity Today*, U.S. prison evangelist Charles Colson writes, "Having worked in hundreds of prisons around the world, I am convinced that this crisis [of crime] will not be resolved by more cops and cells. The only real solution is the cultivation of conscience." People need to be trained to obey their conscience, the same as children must be trained to speak a language. The process begins in the family where parents teach moral precepts, provide good examples, and require responsible behaviour. When that fails to happen, we need to watch out! If parents don't do it, then rock videos, violent films, and a society committed to value-neutral education will.

A recent U.S. best-seller is *The Book of Virtues* by William J. Bennett, former Secretary of Education in Washington. It is an anthology of classic stories and writings that speak of values and virtues, such as self-discipline, compassion, responsibility, friendship, courage, honesty, loyalty, and faith. The success of this book is a hopeful sign, but it is ironic that, in this age, a book with such a title could do so well.

Once, when visiting a church-affiliated school for an Ash Wednesday service, I arrived a little early and found myself wandering down the hall to the principal's office, looking at the plaques on the wall. They contain the names of students who, for a variety of accomplishments,